LAW OF THE LETTER

LAW OF THE LETTER

ELIZABETH GALOOZIS

AN INLANDIA INSTITUTE PUBLICATION

RIVERSIDE, CALIFORNIA

Paperback ISBN: 978-1-955969-42-0
E-Book ISBN: 978-1-955969-43-7

Publications Coordinator: Laura Villareal
Cover Art: Orra White Hitchcock
Book layout & design: David Wojciechowski

Library of Congress Cataloging-in-Publication Data

Names: Galoozis, Elizabeth, author.
Title: Law of the letter / Elizabeth Galoozis.
Other titles: Law of the letter (Compilation)
Description: Riverside, California : Inlandia Institute, 2025. | Summary:
 "In Law of the Letter, Elizabeth Galoozis explores the tension between the natural rhythms
 of the planet and the human urge to enumerate, label, categorize, and neatly organize. Artistic
 and commercial representations of plants clash with their earthier, real-life versions; the
 pandemic and climate change wear down the carefuly-wrought."--
 Provided by publisher.
Identifiers: LCCN 2024052415 (print) | LCCN 2024052416 (ebook) | ISBN 9781955969420
 (paperback) | ISBN 9781955969437 (ebook)
Subjects: LCGFT: Poetry.
Classification: LCC PS3607.A4236 L39 2025 (print) | LCC PS3607.A4236
 (ebook) | DDC 811/.6--dc23/eng/20241105
LC record available at https://lccn.loc.gov/2024052415
LC ebook record available at https://lccn.loc.gov/2024052416

Printed and bound in the United States Distributed by Ingram
Published by Inlandia Institute
Riverside, California
www.InlandiaInstitute.org
First Edition

for Michelle Maso, who embraces all of me

Table of Contents

I. ETYMOLOGY

Law of the Letter

Asking questions got me yelled at.
Better, I learned, not to know the secret but to know it existed,
catch the sound of whispers but not their shapes.
Don't be shitty, dad said to me when I thought I'd make a joke instead.
Eggshells hid under the carpet. I thought it was funny.
Fourth grade, I went to the state spelling bee,
got tripped up on a word I knew, I can never forget–*sachet*.

How cocky I must have become,
I thought later, to rush through such a familiar word. Talk about a
joke. To be ditched by the only dependable
knowledge: the order of letters, so confirmable.
Letters have always soothed me when
my parents couldn't.
No words that can't be put into
order. I loved taking names from the
phone book to alphabetize them, finding the rare ones beginning with
Q. Even now, when I need to sleep or steady myself, I
run through the alphabet. Listing cities, poets, flowers,
skeleton elements, sacred places, systems of belief—anything that can be put
 into order.
The words in their places
unadulterated by silenced or secret meanings.
Visualize their shapes in sensed order, a skill no one
wants anymore. There is spell check; there is sorting column
X, A-Z. There are sentences I can write now:
You don't have to win the spelling bee. You didn't deserve to be yelled at. You
 don't have to finish the list.

On Good Terms

In the restaurant in Greektown,
the trompe l'oeil walls
are painted with decanters,
vines, whitewashed domes
beside a blue sea, islands
where my ancestors
might have trampled grapes.
Waiters bear flaming trays
to Greeks and *exenos* alike.

> The last island my great-grandparents saw
> was Ellis. They lived in dark houses
> where it snowed. Their five sons
> went to work in a steel mill
> that made them cough, and so
> they took up cigarettes and booze.
> Ashtrays everywhere in my grandfather's house,
> the smoke legible in my clothes.
> The booze was blurrier, earlier.

Our waiter tries to speak to me,
but I don't know enough Greek.
Most of the words I picked up
were ones I wasn't supposed to say.
What the laminated menu calls
avgolemono we called "Greek soup,"
traditionally served at my grandparents' table
with Pepsi, saltines, and more ham
than a human could possibly eat.

> The last time I was at their table,
> I was old enough to want a drink
> and old enough to know not to ask.

I'd stopped eating meat
but there was still ham on my plate.
They didn't care if I married a Greek,
but they weren't sure why I wasn't working on it.
If I mentioned you, I used the words
roommate, friend. The peace relied on silence.

A word I know: *metaxa. It's like whiskey,*
I explain. When I tip back
the shot, my throat clenches
and volleys the spirit
onto the table's gorgeous spread.
Tears salt the liquor on my chin.
When I raise the second shot,
I toast to you. My tongue loosened with proof,
I call you my family, say your name.

Black and White

Your lab partner leans down,
listening for some crackle or
hum from your just-constructed battery.
Chalk dust pervades the space.
The black table is ringed in white
from past experiments. Your hand is just
centimeters from hers. This frame
captures one September in
a series: it is always time
to learn about electricity.
Here, everyone is always eleven.
They're always seconds away
from a new understanding,
from learning the intended
lesson or some other unpleasant
or exciting thing, winding into
the brain like a wire, recurring knowledge
vibrating inopportunely:
your dead father. This girl your mother
objects to on sight. The principles
of power. How many minutes remain
in the hour.

Loop

or, using my name against myself

I am all angst,
all the time.
Lists hover over me,
beat through me,
beat me.
I am beat.
I try to make sense
out of the many letters
I answer to.
Too many. A superfluous M
in the middle
to make it even longer.

Am I too loud?
Too zealous?
Too much?
I always take it to heart.
Heart?
Obviously.
Things have gone south before.
They might again.

Lists scroll through me.
Endless. Infinite.
I always take it to heart.
It?
Everything.

Cento: Daddy Issues

My mother dreamed you face down in the sea.
Such a dark funnel, my father!
I see your voice
Black and leafy, as in my childhood.
One day you will love me, even you.
a gradual body
Half remembered, astral with phosphor
He was my Father. I was his son.

Daddy, I have had to kill you.
His last words to Mother were:
"I feel awful."
Always that same old story—
Father Time and Mother Earth,
a marriage on the rocks.

Bleached hull, moon-eaten chain.
Cold worlds shake from the oar.
The spirit of blackness is in us, it is in the fishes.
The coldest darkness sprouts.
This is the sea, this great abeyance.
Starless and fatherless, a dark water.
A drowned man, complaining of the great cold,
Crawls up out of the sea.

This is the end of running on the waves;
We are poured out like water.
The sea was aware
As flowers at the bedside of a wound.
Ashore, the warm waves licked our feet.
And throwing back its head the sea began to sing.
What keyhole have we slipped through, what door has shut?
Old barnacled umbilicus, Atlantic cable,

Keeping itself, it seems, in a state of miraculous repair.
Father, this thick air is murderous.
Daddy, I'm finally through.

They say, "I had my life when I was young."
"Anchors aweigh," Daddy boomed in his bathtub.
Thirty years now I have labored
To dredge the silt from your throat.
Only miniature
Whirlpools, her faint
Ritualistic cries.
The heart shuts,
The sea slides back,
The mirrors are sheeted.

Don't hate your parents, or your children will hire
unknown men to bury you at your own cost.
Old women I hardly remember come up to say my name
And kiss me.
This is not death, it is something safer.
The black telephone's off at the root,
The voices just can't worm through.
Daddy, daddy, you bastard, I'm through.

lines from Sylvia Plath, James Merrill, and Robert Lowell

Cancer Moon, Cancer Rising

the flat sheet of sea
between each wave
has always been a church
for my body.
the place
where I grasp its matter.

my most moving dreams
suffused with water:
gravely shining fish
streaming around me
in a sodden meadow.
bathing in the light
of an outsized moon
pulling at my blood
as it shimmers.

I moved to the ocean
as soon as I could.
then to another.
let myself
be scratched and pummeled
for the joy
of being carried into shore.
let salt lodge
in my throat
for the night.
I have never tried to exert my own power.
even to think I could.
to say to the ocean anything
but
you are my body;
my body is you.

the first time I was depressed

one towel covering me,
another beneath.
neon terry warming
from the climbing sun.

I'm sinking
into the rock,
my cheek
pressed to it.
one ear receives
the thrum of the earth,
the other splashes and laughter.

we rowed to an island
unsupervised.
jumping topless
into the lake.
I am
too heavy for it.

I don't want to die
or live.
the hours
are as mute as I am.
what is there
to be sad about?

I am
a volcanic stone,
something to leap from,
rest beside,
drape your bathing suit over.
I don't want to move
or stay.

my friends
don't question
or worry me.
when the sun
begins sinking,
they use their weight
to lift me,
warm and strong.

Symbol of Affection

We were piling the crunchy leaves
to fall on, kicking the still-bright ones
into momentary, sunlit arcs.
Her arms out for a hug,
she touched her left hand with her right,
face folding as she surveyed the park.

She enlisted us in searching.
Other parents came to help,
squatting and crumbling dead leaves,
dismantling the hills and crevices we'd made.

Someone else's husband found it,
plucked the thing
from the roots of a pine
and tucked it into my mother's hand,
closed her fingers over it.
Her expression relief,
changing to something dull,
resigned, as she slid the ring
onto her own finger
under a bower of trees on fire.

The Branches Regard the Tree

You began with impromptu lessons
about acceptable mates, pointing out
the car window: no tattoos,
no smoking, no one like *that*.
(Like what?)
Later, oblique rules
meant as barricades:
keep my door open
and my feet on the floor.
Be home by eleven;
only sleep over
with other girls.

I thought it was all mine
to unmake.
The relief of splitting
from conviction mine
to feel,
sliding into a backseat
under my own supervision.

But you hemmed yourself in, too.
Gave in to painful
ramifications.
I didn't grow away
fast enough, didn't predict
the dissonant crack
across the limbs
that was always coming.

riding my bike drunk at twenty-three

the wet street littered
with melting hail
from last night's storm
and petals,
torn and smashed,
indecent shades of magenta.
everything saturated.

keep it together
until you get home:
that transitory
narrow bed
a port in a storm,
windows cracked.

keep it together.
this is surely
the way home.

stop sign.
a fallen sapling's roots
sideways
and dripping.
my hands too slow to
brake altogether.

what if I hadn't had
too many?
what if I'd had
a baby?
what if I'd taken off
with someone
or to somewhere

instead of returning
to the town I grew up in
for no reason
other than it was there?
the plainest fig
on the tree,
the lowest.
every other rotted fruit
crushed beneath my wheels.

you have got
to keep it together.

stop, too hard.
it's the same sign.
I swear
I knew where I was going.
why can't I just get home?

keep it together.
this time, turn the other way.
this time,
flowers climb the wall
in yellow semaphore:
you have time.
you can stop.
just wait
until you get home.

II. SILENT LETTERS

dispersal

a symposium of seeds
climbs on the gusts
shaking the cypresses
and satellite dishes,

lands to be flattened
by a work boot.
skitters, sciurine,
to a patch of dirt. it is hard
to admit rancor.
to decide whether
we want to be noticed.
to expose our skin
to the detritus the wind carries.
to bear its sharp breath.
to heed the trochees of the window
knocking against
its own frame, saying:
enter, enter, enter.

Memorial Hill

Young and easy under the changing leaves, earnest
as the quad was green.
Words poured from our green fingers
as if they'd never stop, as if
we'd never be at a loss. Our words
meant everything. Each other's words.
Every word was gold.
We stayed all night
at the library,
passing paper and climbing
the wide bright stairs.
Reading "Fern Hill" and "Ariel,"
letting their poets' youth bless us
and their doomed youth
wash over us.

I danced, watched others dance,
watched you dance like you never told me
your trouble. I shouldered you home, only
a little less drunk than you.
Watched the sun rise
from the top of Memorial Hill,
lighting the soccer fields and woods,
the war memorial and its carved names,
in green and gold.
Those young people
who would never get old.

Light and dark rushed in where we let them.
Time pushed us, green and fighting,
to parse harsh words at distance.
I deliberately forgot the words
we shared, the words

that meant everything.
The green and the gold behind me.

Ten years you and I
slowly followed time into grace,
into each other's graces.
The grass, the monuments,
the pages, lost their sharpness
in receding.

When we finally meet again,
it's over whiskey
at the White Horse Tavern.
We leave strutting, chanting:

Dylan Thomas, motherfuckers,
Dylan Thomas! Poor
Dylan Thomas, slipping
unconscious into legend,
mourning his youth
a final time. We are still
only thirty, our words
more polished every year.
Stumbling from the street,
but stumbling forward.

Quabbin Reservoir

The perimeter is paved
for people like us
to drive through
and take pictures.
Wide, deep water
submerging four dissolved towns:
dismantled libraries,
vacated graves,
abandoned rooms where couples slept together,
so the rest of the commonwealth
could cook and bathe and drink.

You pull over, suddenly
recognizing your own unmarked attraction.
Lead me into the woods
to show me what was once a house.
Boggy steps slump
to the sunken leaf-layered hollow
that was the cellar.
I won't go so far
as to descend them.

Around the next bend,
the observation tower.
At the top,
we press our faces to the glass.
Our arms touching from shoulder to wrist,
we lean on years of carved names.
Islands that were hills
rise below us.
We stay, close, a long time.

It's dark as I drive, alone,
back to Boston: pragmatic, alive,
beside a breathing ocean,
its monuments preserved.
The moon is half-visible
and half-obscured.
At home,
high above the street,
I turn the tap.
Water has also traveled
from there to here,
from the watershed we observed
to my outstretched hands.

Resorts

They are always
at the lip of a cliff,
up an impassable mountain
or down a flammable canyon.
The places where,
supine in daytime,
we order tart, boozy drinks.

The places where
we build steam rooms in the tropics
and saunas in the desert.
Half-eaten plates of fries are cleaned
from the poolside tables.
Dead leaves are gleaned
from the pool.
Paint, brooms, hammers;
so much labor to preserve
what could disintegrate so quickly.
Given time
plus dirt,
plus rot,
plus fire,
plus buckled roads.
Useless keycards will litter
the floor; the gates they opened
will collapse. No one
will rate the cleanliness of sheets;
no one will apologize
for how long it took
to make your margarita.
Every view will be
a mountain view.
Palm trees will tower higher,

nourished by repossessed water
that—for now—
you float in
on a holiday no one will mark,
the one where we're thankful
that we occupied land
to make better use of it.
Where speakers hidden in the succulents
issue Judy Garland's plaintive words
already attending to the future,
and you sing along:
next year,
all our troubles
will be out of sight.

The Grove

Third & Fairfax, Los Angeles

A thick, slow crowd, oozing
out and in the openings,
pulled by gleam
and split by artificial branches.

Everything relentlessly tasteful and shiny.
The fountains drown the sounds of birds,
our quiet conversation, all pleas
and thank-yous.

We wanted to come here,
knowing only the name. A grove with
only trees in cages, a "Farmers' Market"
with no farmers.

Laden and lonely
under the fluorescents,
reflected in a hundred makeup mirrors,
our energy's sapped.

The gleaming trolley
takes us the half-mile
we can't seem to walk.
Buy something. Shell out

because we're far from home:
everyone is. It takes ten minutes
to get to a street with traffic,
the actual smell of oil.

Carry That Weight

Washed-out clouds press, hard
and too close, onto our heads,
against the mountains.

I press my lips to
George Harrison's head, gazing
across Abbey Road.

I've crossed that road too—
a more "Here Comes the Sun" time
than "She's So Heavy."

Fruit litters the ground;
it's made itself too heavy
to bear its own flesh.

George is long gone, but
his words keep coming around
to bear the silence.

No humans around.
Lizards skitter; smaller birds
dive-bomb unmoved crows.

At dusk, a small plane
unloads its sound, passing low,
toward the small airfield.

The moon loads the light
it unloaded just last month,
waxing lyrical.

That magic feeling,
nowhere to go. But the months
keep coming around.

In the Rothko Chapel

The giant paintings
look black at first,
the deep violet revealed
only through
sustained attention,
acclimation to
the low light.

> The labor
> is visible
> when you
> get close.

I remember the moment
I realized I loved Rothko.
I thought I knew what I loved
(detail, precision)
and what I didn't
(wordless walls of color, an emotion
rendered so completely
it can't be ignored).

> I have words
> inked into my arm
> that I have loved
> a long time.

The stone floor
takes heat
from my body.

> My body is mine
> but I wanted you
> to have it.

The first painting of his
I loved:

warm satsuma
and gold.
My body warmed
to it.

I wanted
you
to have it.

I wanted
to forget words.

I have words
inked into
my arm
that you love.

These paintings,
somber indigo,
absorb heat.

The labor
is visible
when you
get close.

Heat seeps
from my body
into the stone floor.
I sit
a long time.

I have words
inked
into my arm
that I love.

I thought I knew
I only loved
what could be described.
Then I knew
I loved
Rothko.
No less beautiful

because I couldn't explain.

The labor
is painfully
visible.

I wanted it.
I wanted warm
satsuma and gold.
But violet-dark
is only cold
if I only feel
the surface
of my body.

Alone
in silence
I admit
what I've felt.

Heat finds
its level.

The words
made visible.

Path Between Amherst and Northampton

Pedaling, the cliché
       is true: the body knows the way still,
    the inner, weightless skill
of balancing on the steel seat,
dry fingers taut and light
       on the handlebars, like reading
    the brakes' quick pulse. The thing,
simpler than recalled—moving, but
with almost no effort—
       lifts the pressure you exert: what
    yoga promises, not
in lengthened salutation, but from
       the heart leaping, lissome,
    from the body (toward the sun) and
ahead of its rest and
       motion. The easing of sorrow.
    Ahead, the path narrows
to a point closer and closer.
       Streaking down the greener-
    gold tunnel, lit from either side,
the thought appears, collides
       as if tossed from a tree, skyed like
    a stone into the bike:
the less painful, swifter flight through
       this space is movement through
    time, too. The minutes pass you now
like the trees, and you see how
       in the future, at the route's end,
    approaching always, stands
the person missed, beloved, and
       reunion at hand,
    nearer every cycle and each
push, coming into reach.

III. CONTRACTIONS

My Wife Falls Asleep to *Friends* and it Streams All Night

And I'm left awake
to decide when to mute the timeline:
maybe, the one
where they swap apartments
of radically different shape and quality
in the same building,
or the one
where everyone has a good laugh
about how silly Phoebe is
to follow her mother's advice
when the woman killed herself, lol.

The next morning,
Monica and Chandler may be married,
but that night,
they will still be arguing
about the wedding.
The next morning,
Rachel's teeth
are blinding in their fabricated uniformity,
but that night,
they soften
into the mouth of a common person.
All the jokes
that unwound silently over us
as we slept
recursively find their sound
the next evening:
Joey tries wearing women's underwear,
but stops because it makes him seem gay.
Chandler enjoys watching red carpets,
but hides it

because it makes him seem gay.
Ross curls himself around Joey in a nap,
and everyone runs to see for themselves
because it makes them seem gay.
Kathleen Turner shows up as Chandler's drag queen dad,
and everyone loses their minds.

Every twenty-five minutes
they are twenty-five again,
splashing around in a fountain
on the Warner Brothers lot,
dancing according to their archetypes
twenty times a night
and forever.

[quarantine]

The air in our third-floor apartment
was wet
and heavy.
All my senses
observed it acutely
until they filled.
I walked downstairs,
opened the mailbox
with its small key.
Sat on a narrow ledge
outside the building,
reading a letter from a friend
and shuffling the rest,
buying time.
The sun drew my face
up and away from words.
All at once
I remembered
the complete pleasure
of being alone,
free of even a sensed presence
in the next room.
And the other soothing pleasure
of being alone
in a crowd,
on a street or train,
my own energy growing
from going my own way
among everyone else
going theirs.

elemental

I. air/fire
the lungs ask
to take air,
no matter how ruined.
if the window is closed
to wildfire ash,
what's in here?
what is breathed
by the cat,
the money plant,
the unguarded lung?

burning a candle
feels like a violent act.
my nose bleeds.
the petaled clusters
that make up the lungs
bloom and fold.
atom by atom,
the air inside
and outside
transposing.

the universe, mostly air,
traverses our bodies
while it can.

II. water/earth
at last, it rains.
by evening
disappeared into sidewalk cracks,
taken up with alarming speed
by roots near the surface,
evaporated from metal benches
painted with sunset-colored poppies,
absorbed into fountains and pools
miles from mountain lakes.

a drop wakes us.
over us, the gray ceiling
distends unnaturally
in natural shapes:
horsetail, nimbus.
from the largest and roundest,
a slow drip of amber liquid
makes a sick attempt to nourish.
by morning, they've formed patterns:
galaxy, virus.
they swell and recede.

outside, the roots are dry again.
the sun presses itself
against the flammable hills;
the desert beneath us
waits to take it all back.

[quarantine]

There is sky in the door—
Easter blue
fading up
to gold-red clouds.
The window only gazes
onto other windows.
The top of the head
must be lifted off
to dissipate negative
and undermining thoughts.
One can only stretch
so far.
A star shape
of the body
abuts the furniture.
A pirouette
knocks a book from the shelf.
A single wine glass
sits reused, unclinked.
There is earth in the ceiling.
The walls press
so.

Missing Gridlock

Each mile
brings me closer
to the Arctic Circle,
bright halo of the planet
weeping ice.
Several screens
tell me how cold it is,
how fast I am,
the limit to how fast
I can be.
I am beginning to tire
of gray highways,
of the glut and spread
of Walmarts and Dunkin's and Chili's.
To tire of never getting to stop
at lights or in traffic
to dine on the dramas
through other car windows:
laughter
and singing
and other elements
of surviving.

[quarantine]

On the mornings we're both here and awake
I steam oat milk in your favorite mug.
Into it, I pour the pulled shots.
This is known as marking the foam.

The mug is one I've managed not to break.
Not to mention all I've left unplugged,
the cheesecake you worked so hard on that I forgot
on the counter overnight, sweating under its dome.

What streams to us alternates
among period pieces, true crime, real housewives slinging mud.
We wake up cold and go to bed hot,
to dramas of our own.

We sleep to reruns, wake
to crabs or pugs
in human clothes with human plots.
The pillow, the remote, the water glass, the phones.

Your lunches for the week are made.
You've uprooted the bathroom clog.
It's been a week since we last fought.
I'm writing you into a poem.

espresso cup

too small for the dishwasher,
it slipped the top rack
and cracked
into what at first
seemed like reparable pieces.
the words *bon marché*
split on the outside,
rive gauche on the bottom.
tan water line of the shot
still visible.

the year of planning,
of saving money,
of convincing ourselves we deserved
what better-off friends
did fifteen years ago:
fly to London
and take a train to Paris
and climb elegantly tiled escalators
to choose this tiny vessel
for a daily ritual.

to remind myself
every morning
in this plague year
that once, we boarded airplanes.
once, we walked on a crowded street
following signs with unfamiliar words,
spending other currencies,
clinking cups gently,
turning our bare faces to the sun.

[quarantine]

No one uses words
like "displeased" or "inconvenience."
Every objection is inflamed and serious,
insistent and religious.
We keep our conversations sparse
in case they bloom to violence.

We know this before speaking.
One of the few things we can know.
Like the beating of dough under our hands,
or the ticking of the clock,
or pretending that taking walks
is just as good as flying to Tokyo.

On our latest,
we stand under the bridge
where (though it was still being built)
dozens of people jumped
after the crash
a hundred years ago.

There was no seeing beyond
the plunging numbers,
the lines for bread.
No sense for the future.

One of the bodies, they say,
fell into the concrete,
remains part
of the muscular central column.

Have Yourself

Christmas Eve
at the Stater Brothers
on Foothill
in the year of our lord
(lord, it is still)
2020.
I am trying to remember
the ingredients for a simple recipe,
which I could search for
on the computer in my pocket,
but I can't admit
one more unknowable thing.
I must know without looking
what I need,
where to find it,
and how to get back to the house
I have lived in for two days.
I've been in here too long already.

A lone man sways
in the liquor aisle,
breathing damply out
his uncovered nose.
Over the speaker,
the worst versions
of the worst Christmas songs.
I can't place the generic voices.

At checkout,
my face trembles.
I try to focus
on the tender push
of blood out the heart.

In the slick, dark parking lot,
a delivery truck
crosses my path slowly,
gives me plenty of time
to read the name
of my best friend
painted inexplicably
on its side.

Behind the wheel,
I sob from the chest.
I want
my mother.
I want
to touch a person.
I want
the followers of Jesus
to protect the rest of us
as we protect them.
I want
to know when I will know again.
When the moment will arrive
when I can once again
let my heart
be light.

Remembering the Future

"Despair is a confident memory of the future."
— Rebecca Solnit

That time is linear
is a rock in the shoe.
Physicists can insist
that in our universe,
a particle of light goes left,
and in a parallel one,
it goes right.
But who lives there?
Who could tell?

Confidence—
that we will live another day,
that we will not,
that there is only
winning or losing
and nothing halfway—
is offensive to the universe.

It lets us off the hook,
whether our own individual hook
is ornamental and light
or rusty
and heavy,
crawling with worms.

That time is linear
is a crack in the wall.

a cricket in the apartment

we know it
only by its sound,
the vibration of its wings
in the dark.

we have tried
to trace the chirp,
trap it.
closed all the windows,
taken a broom to the skylight
to shake it loose,
but all that fell
was plaster.

it showed up
the day of the election
and has stayed with us
through the counting.

we have tried to be still.
to distinguish its hum
from sirens,
idling engines,
helicopter blades,
incoherent yelling
about stolen votes.

hoping
to starve it out,
we have looked up
what crickets eat.
turns out,
everything: mites, wood, leaves;

fabric, particularly soiled;
anything rotting or dying.
even each other,
even alive.

stuck with it,
stuck with each other,
stuck inside.
the matte black
of the skylight
apes a star-filled summer night,
clink of many sweaty glasses
and a chorus of crickets,
free from daylight predators
and singing.
a small, shining emblem of luck.

IV. COMMON LANGUAGE

Cento: Six Women in Five Parts

I.
A poem can begin
with a lie.

my tools are the wrong ones
for what I have to do.

To be frank,
my muse left town and is much happier now

Open the book.
Open the heavy book.

I don't even have to steal
your words, you give them to me for free

choose any ones you wish
write us a poem.

II.
We are driving to the interior.

A woman lies buried under me,
interred for centuries, presumed dead.
You, who have often made the unnameable
nameable for others, even for me.
You are androgynous and omnipotent.

this then
is the lens
to magnify
ignite

redeem
these words, these whispers, conversations
from which time after time the truth breaks moist and green

we could lay our losses
side-by-side, two gifts
the ocean dragged in.

one of us born again
with a brand-new address or poem
two women, eye to eye
                  a whole new poetry beginning here.

By this rising
some piece of our labor
is already half-done.

Once open the books, you have to face
the underside of everything you've loved.

What kind of beast would turn its life into words?

III.
I have known
all along that
words will not do.
These words
they are stones in the water
running away.

It was an old theme even for me:
Language cannot do everything
and the past echoing through our bloodstreams
is freighted with different language, different meanings

The present breaks our hearts.
But we, we live so much in these
configurations of the past
we drift
separate and syllabic
if we survive at all.

You can't derange, or re-arrange,
your poems again.
The words won't change again.

IV.
I can't name love now
without naming its object
the trees look so queer and green
It took me a time to light the fire.

Until we find each other, we are alone.

If I could let you know—
two women together is a work
nothing in civilization has made simple

Words to a woman, joy
flying wherever
it feels like, gay!

V.
I can't believe you are gone
out of my life
so you are not.

I have wanted one thing: to know
   simply as I know my name
at any given moment, where I stand.

I felt: you are an *I*,
you are an *Elizabeth*,
you are one of *them*.

Step lightly   all around us
words are cracking

Not just the message but the sound.
It's green
and has come to live.

I have to cast my lot with those
who age after age, perversely,
with no extraordinary power,
reconstitute the world.

lines from Gloria Anzaldúa, Elizabeth Bishop, June Jordan,
Audre Lorde, Maggie Nelson, and Adrienne Rich

multiply

we have been flush
this whole time.
bills folded
into one-inch squares,
bound
by flaking rubber bands,
buried
under a vase in pink packing peanuts.

growth
has been happening
this whole time.

seeds
knocked into the yard
root, bloom,
pull monarchs in
on their way to Michoacán.

under the hairy fig and guava branches
creepers take umbrage,
wait.
time in their vessels.

in and under the boxes
in the closets and garage
generations of spiders
ebb and flow.

there is no calm
that does not shelter
furious motion.

how did you get together?

one day our friend asked me why
I didn't have a crush on you.
I didn't
and then I did.
we joked about kissing
and then it wasn't a joke.

it was winter,
the tops of your legs cold
when you took off your jeans.
I didn't know
you never wear pants at home
in any season.

home
began as a gamble.
we took the bus
from the airport
and had our pants off
before we even saw the bedroom.

every night since
we've gotten into the same bed.
unconsciously coupling
our legs
somehow generating heat
in stasis.

Comfort and Joy

All I wanted for Christmas
is the comically round-eyed
look of alarm
my stepmother is giving my father
each time
my niece opens the drawer
of her new toy cash register
and says to me,
how can I help you, sir?

Mabon

for B, K, and L

The bright young circle we once were
re-forms in a half-light, half-dark time,
to channel reaped light from all of us
to the sickness in one of us.
The first dark bloom
whose spread
we will become accustomed to
in twenty years, maybe ten.

We think we knew better
than women in the dark ages
who built harvest altars,
entreating the sun to return.
We have been so certain
we will see another spring.

Now, we form a ring
around her.
We utter words of succor and supplication.
A few grays reflect
the light just starting to fail.

On Wanting to Text the Dead

Today I had ten minutes for lunch
between two committee meetings
and ate grocery-store sushi at my desk,
and when I pulled off the plastic lid,
the soy sauce was missing.
And I thought of the sticky packets
in the back of your desk drawer,
when I was fifteen
and you hired me
to pack your office
and move it down the hall.
I understood the file drawers of journals
and awards that needed dusting
but was confounded
by the soy sauce, aspirin,
airline toothbrushes and combs,
wet-naps long dried out.

Now, I am a person
in an office, and I understand
what is useful to keep in one's desk
That you might have to eat lunch
between committee meetings,
why you sometimes rolled your eyes
before committee meetings.
All I want
is to text you offhandedly,
with the cry-laugh emoji
and maybe one of a tuna roll.
To say thank you
for paying me for my work,
for trusting me to cull and organize,
for modeling a life
for me to imagine.

Pass Me the Ladder

Can I help you?
I'm sorry
the man in charge
is unavailable.
He is always unavailable
in some form or another.

You will find the books about you
under "sexual minorities."
I can help you.
Let us build
knowledge together.

"You will remember
I was not
a Sweet Girl Graduate
of a Library School."*
I am never allowed
to forget.
The men in charge
call themselves
information scientists,
control
uncontrollable ideas
and feelings.
Like depression—

like
of wages.

Like how we are handmaidens
not only to historians
but to our peers
flirting with students
and churning out books
of their own.

Honestly,
fuck
right
off.

You can't build monuments
when you're pulling at seams.
This place
may not be of my own making,
but by Jessamyn West and Audre Lorde
I can smash its walls,
lean my ladder
on your fist.

Nine of Pentacles

now we have
these trees.
not planted by us
but in our care.
well…
your care.
you water them assiduously;
I just sit
on the back patio
with a glass of rum at dusk
under the crescent moon
and watch
with love.

I watch the green fruit form,
its skin distend
and turn yellow
and orange,
swell and cradle its seeds.
so that birds eat them
and shit them out somewhere,
so that there can be more trees,
more fruit,
more trees.

more fruit
for me to pluck
and squeeze into my rum
as I sit under the half-moon
and gaze up
through the leaves.

the bugs that don't bite me
or stick their heads
in the trees' blossoms
rub their legs together
and make
the only sound around.

the word *deserve* means
nothing around here.
the bees and seeds
don't know their labor
ends in a glass of rum,
in the stomach
of an animal
whose shit can't even help them
continue the line.

we don't deserve it.
but we don't not.
the fruit won't be here forever.

mutual aid

for Caro

we will make a place in the desert for us.
for the gray survivors
of every kind of violence,
natural or human.
there,
we will find
and tend
wellsprings, resilient plants.
grow out our wild hair
or cut it all off.
listen to
and say
whatever we want,
including
nothing.
make a table
we all want to eat from.
make dark rooms
to rest in the peak of the sun.
leach out the residues,
the microparticles of pollution,
of our former lives,
from our blood and breath.
hold each other's hands
and say,
we're
here
now.

Notes

Thank you to Katie Baker for the Dylan Thomas stories (and so much else!) in "Memorial Hill."

"Resorts" contains a line from "Have Yourself a Merry Little Christmas" (written by Hugh Martin and Ralph Blane).

The epigraph for "Remembering the Future" comes from Rebecca Solnit's essay "Woolf's Darkness," which I read in her collection *Men Explain Things to Me*.

"Carry That Weight" contains a line from "You Never Give Me Your Money" (Lennon-McCartney).

I encountered the story of Charles Lummis (referenced in "Pass Me the Ladder") in Susan Orlean's *The Library Book*. This poem also owes a debt to Caro Pinto for the Zen story (which I haven't been able to find the origin of) about leaning your ladder against another wall.

The lines in "Cento: Daddy Issues" come from (in order of appearance): "Electra on Azalea Path" and "Little Fugue" (Sylvia Plath); "Pieces of History" and "Swimming by Night" (James Merrill); "Dunbarton" (Robert Lowell); "Daddy" (Plath); "Terminal Days at Beverly Farms" (Lowell); "The Broken Home" and "The Summer People" (Merrill); "Crossing the Water" (Plath); "Accumulations of the Sea" (Merrill); "Berck-Plage," "Sheep in Fog," and "A Life" (Plath); "The Quaker Graveyard in Nantucket" (Lowell); "The Drowning Poet" and "The Parrot Fish" (Merrill); "The Babysitters," "Lesbos," "Full Fathom Five," and "Daddy" (Plath); "Mother and Father I" and "Commander Lowell" (Lowell); "The Colossus" (Plath); "The Current" (Merrill); "Contusion" (Plath); "The Hard Way" (Lowell); "Pieces of History" (Merrill); "Poem for a Birthday" and "Daddy" (Plath).

The lines in "Cento: Six Women in Five Parts" come from (in order of appearance): "Cartographies of Silence" and "The Roofwalker" (Adrienne Rich); "The Latest Winter" (Maggie Nelson); "Over 2,000 Illustrations and a Complete

Concordance" (Elizabeth Bishop); "The Mute November" (Nelson); "Prism" (Audre Lorde); "Arrival at Santos" (Bishop); "A Woman Lies Buried Under Me" (Gloria Anzaldúa); "Twenty-One Love Poems" (Rich); "Words to a Woman" (Nelson); "6.3.96-6.4.96" (June Jordan); "Cartographies of Silence" (Rich); "Father's Day" (Nelson); "Girlfriend" (Lorde); "Transcendental Etude" (Rich); "Today is Not the Day" (Lorde); "Twenty-One Love Poems" (Rich); "Poem Written In Someone Else's Office" (Nelson); "These Poems" (Jordan); "Cartographies of Silence," "Twenty-One Love Poems," "Readings of History," and "Splittings" (Rich); "Thaw" (Lorde); "North Haven" (Bishop); "First Things" (Rich); "Letter to N.Y." (Bishop); "I Had to Go Down" (Anzaldúa); "Hunger" and "Twenty-One Love Poems" (Rich); "Words to a Woman" (Nelson); "Sonnet" (Bishop); "Lunar Eclipse" and "Double Monologue" (Rich); "In the Waiting Room" (Bishop); "Thaw" (Rich); "Problems of Translation: Problems of Language" (Jordan); "Saturday Morning" (Nelson); "Natural Resources" (Rich).

Acknowledgements

These poems appeared in the following publications, some in different forms:

Air/Light: "Law of the Letter," "My Wife Falls Asleep to Friends and it Streams All Night," and "Quabbin Reservoir"

aurora journal: "Cancer Moon, Cancer Rising"

Call Me [Brackets]: "Pass Me the Ladder" and "Path Between Amherst and Northampton"

Faultline Journal of Arts and Letters: "Mabon"

Gathering: A Women Who Submit Anthology (Jamii Publishing): "mutual aid"

horse egg literary: "a cricket in the apartment"

in parentheses: "Resorts"

The Indianapolis Review: "In the Rothko Chapel"

Inverted Syntax: "The Grove"

miniskirt magazine: "[quarantine]" (page 42) as "Quarantine Poem #5"

Painted Bride Quarterly: "Missing Gridlock"

RHINO: "Black and White"

Sinister Wisdom: "The Branches Regard the Tree" and "Memorial Hill":

Sundog Lit: "Cento: Six Women in Five Parts"

Sweet: "Dispersal"

Transformation: A Women Who Submit Anthology (Jamii Publishing): "multiply"

Witness : "Nine of Pentacles"

Gratitude

A first book necessitates a long list of thanks; this book would not exist without any of the following people and organizations. My communities are home-grown and deep-rooted, and I am infinitely grateful to every one of you.

Deepest thanks to Megan Gravendyk-Estrella for selecting my book for this prize, and to Laura Villareal and Cati Porter at Inlandia for guiding me through the publication process and answering my many questions. An endless well of gratitude to Claire Wahmanholm, who worked with me to shape and sequence a mere collection of poems into a real book. With empathy and incisiveness, you helped me see where I wanted to go even when I didn't know–the mark of a great mentor. Thank you to the AWP Writer to Writer Mentoring Program for pairing us and to Micaela Tore for facilitating our partnership. Thank you to Claire, along with Xochitl-Julisa Bermejo and Sebastian Merrill, for generously providing blurbs.

I restarted my dreams of publishing poems at the age of thirty-six. When I joined Women Who Submit in 2020, it changed my life. I've learned so much from the writers and leaders in this kickass organization, and I'm proud to be a part of it. Thank you, Xochitl-Julisa Bermejo, for creating and leading this community. Particular thanks go to WWS members Suhasini Yeeda, Juanita E. Mantz, Lauren Eggert-Crowe, Daria Topousis, Lisa Cheby, Laura Sturza, Lisbeth Coiman, Désirée Zamorano, and fellow Inlandia author Tisha Marie Reichle-Aguilera. Women Who Submit materially supported my work through the Ashaki M. Jackson No Barriers Grant, which covered several submission fees.

Abby Saunders Nolin: you also changed my life by asking me one day at lunch almost ten years ago if I'd like to join a writers' group. Since then, I've had the pleasure of getting to know a ridiculously talented group of people and their work; their feedback shaped many of these poems. Along with Abby, thank you to past and present members for conversations, laughs, and support: Julie Cohen, Robyn Wilson, Babs Gray, Anna Perez, Alex Jospin, Robyn Morrison, Rebecca Snavely, Matt Siegel, Amber Bansak, Brad Cheyne, Leonard Hyman, and Shannon Davis. I'm also grateful to Julie Adamo, Jules FitzGerald, Adam Rosenkranz, and Reyna Grande for feedback and conversations about writing, and to the Facebook group Binders Full of Women and Non-Binary Poets—the best corner of the Internet.

Many of these poems were written during the strange and lonely time of the pandemic, when my cat Stella finally warmed to me and kept me company. I was sustained in those months by artists who generously shared their art and hope through social media, particularly Indigo Girls, Ryan Heffington, and DJ D-Nice.

My time at Amherst College was spent in a community of teachers, students, and staff who expanded my literary horizons and ambitions. You are many, but I specifically want to thank Sam Masinter, Evan Klavon, Edward A. Farmer, David Molina, Katherine Duke, Catherine Newman, and David Sofield. Thank you to Maryanne Alos, Daria D'Arienzo, and Judy Lively at Frost Library for the best job on campus. Thank you to Judith Frank for being the best advisor a first-year could have; you made me feel at home right away. There aren't enough thanks in the world for Daniel Hall— thesis advisor, teacher, ultimate dinner host, and friend—who gave me two pieces of advice I think about all the time: "There should always be at least two things going on in a poem," and "You have to order a specific brand of alcohol; otherwise, they'll serve you rotgut." Thank you to Laura Schuyler for inviting me to my first open mic at Marsh Coffee House, and to all the friends who came to listen to my words, but especially Joanne Kang, Katelyn Gamson, Jenn Morash Scott, Barbara Sieck, and Katie Baker.

Endless gratitude to Laura Younkin, my first librarian hero and a gem of a human being, who created a safe space at a high school in Louisville for the weird, creative, and queer kids. Thanks and love to Rebecca Tedesco, one of my first and most thoughtful readers. I cherish our friendship, conversations about creativity and learning, and the way you've kept it real with me for almost thirty years.

Thank you to all the physical and mental health practitioners who have cared for me and helped me navigate chronic illness—especially the neurology departments at Brigham and Women's in Boston and Keck Medicine of USC in LA. Lynn Bratman and Nancy Parson—I would never have the courage to have written most of this without you.

This book is shaped by the writers I presumptuously think of as my literary ancestors—Elizabeth Bishop, Audre Lorde, Sylvia Plath, Adrienne Rich, and Virginia Woolf. Their words have saved me again and again.

Caro Pinto— my *consigliere*, my ride or die, my platonic soulmate—there are too many things to thank you for, but I know you know. We truly found love in a hopeless place.

Thank you to all of my families—Galoozis, Imber, Bracker, Hill, and Maso. I'm lucky to be a part of you, and I love how we can simultaneously celebrate and rib each other. My sister, Christina, and I have exchanged words—sharp, funny, heartfelt—our whole lives. You're the only one who speaks the same language I do. My mother, Lisa, took us to the public library every week and nurtured our love of reading and writing. Thank you for always being my biggest champion, supporting all of my dreams, and giving me not just life, but a beautiful life. My stepfather, Jeff, was in my life for a short time but had, as he would say, a "huge" impact on me. Whenever I hesitate to take a risk, I hear him cheering me on.

Finally: how can I begin to thank my wife, Michelle? You've stuck by me in emergency rooms and cross-country moves, and through disappointments, adventures, triumphs, and domestic moments of joy. You give me space to write and read, and to laugh and rest. Thank you for making dinner on Tuesday nights and for the thousands of thoughtful gestures and moments of grace you've shown me. We're kind of the best, and everyone else should be jealous.

ABOUT ELIZABETH GALOOZIS

Law of the Letter is ELIZABETH GALOOZIS's first full-length collection, and the regional winner of the Hillary Gravendyk Prize from the Inlandia Institute. She writes about lineage, language, and queerness, and her work has appeared in *RHINO*, *Air/Light*, *Sinister Wisdom*, *Painted Bride Quarterly*, *Witness*, and elsewhere. Elizabeth has been nominated twice for a Pushcart Prize and once for Best of the Net, and was selected by Claire Wahmanholm for AWP's Writer to Writer Program in 2022. Elizabeth has roots in the Midwest and New England, and now lives in southern California with her wife, Michelle. She can be found at @thisamericanliz, and at www.elizabethgaloozis.com.

ABOUT INLANDIA INSTITUTE

The Inlandia Institute is a regional literary non-profit and publishing house. We seek to bring focus to the richness of the literary enterprise that has existed in this region for ages.

The mission of Inlandia Books is to recognize, support, and expand literary activity in Inland Southern California by publishing works which deepen people's awareness, understanding, and appreciation of this unique, complex and creatively vibrant region. The mission is carried out by actively seeking out new works by writers who are affiliated with the region, and also through national literary competitions which elevate Inlandia Books to the national literary stage.

To learn more about the Inlandia Institute, please visit our website at www.InlandiaInstitute.org.

pain survey by Jennifer MacKenzie
Winner of the 2023 National Hillary Gravendyk Prize

The artemisia by William S. Barnes
Winner of the 2022 National Hillary Gravendyk Prize

Bones Awaiting the Blaze by Tiffany Elliott
Winner of the 2022 Regional Hillary Gravendyk Prize

How to Know You're Dreaming When You're Dreaming
by Angelica Maria Barraza Tran
Winner of the 2021 National Hillary Gravendyk Prize

Our Lady of Perpetual Desert by Alexandra Martinez
Winner of the 2021 Regional Hillary Gravendyk Prize

among the enemies by Michael Samra
Winner of the 2020 National Hillary Gravendyk Prize

This Side of the Fire by Jonathan Maule
Winner of the 2020 Regional Hillary Gravendyk Prize

The Silk the Moths Ignore by Bronwen Tate
Winner of the 2019 National Hillary Gravendyk Prize

Remyth: A Postmodernist Ritual by Adam Martinez
Winner of the 2019 Regional Hillary Gravendyk Prize

Former Possessions of the Spanish Empire by Michelle Peñaloza
Winner of the 2018 National Hillary Gravendyk Prize

All the Emergency-Type Structures by Elizabeth Cantwell
Winner of the 2018 Regional Hillary Gravendyk Prize

Our Bruises Kept Singing Purple by Malcolm Friend
Winner of the 2017 National Hillary Gravendyk Prize

Traces of a Fifth Column by Marco Maisto
Winner of the 2016 National Hillary Gravendyk Prize

God's Will for Monsters by Rachelle Cruz
Winner of the 2016 Regional Hillary Gravendyk Prize
Winner of the 2018 American Book Award

Map of an Onion by Kenji C. Liu
Winner of the 2015 National Hillary Gravendyk Prize

All Things Lose Thousands of Times by Angela Peñaredondo
Winner of the 2015 Regional Hillary Gravendyk Prize